D1790889

Arizona Cooking

I

© 2001 by Barbara Soden

To the people of Arizona, that wonderful state. Here are a few recipes from our corner of the world.

NOTES:

TABLE OF CONTENTS

ARIZONA COOKING

The first time I flew into Phoenix I was in love with Arizona. The view from the plane was one of contrasts and colors. The pink and purple mountains majesty surrounds the sparkling valley. There are stark deserts, with a variety of cacti and other desert plants and large cities that reflect the state's growth.

It is the 48th state in the union, founded in 1912 and in its' 80+ years there has been tremendous growth.

(continued)

Phoenix, it's capital, grows by the thousands every month, people flock here to enjoy the warm winters and the spectacular views.

Tucson, Flagstaff, Prescott are all booming cities and all are equal in their beauty. Then of course, there is the Grand Canyon, a sight to behold. To describe it would not do it justice.

Now you know, I love Arizona and want you to enjoy some of the wonderful recipes that come from this part of the country. Enjoy!

NOTES:

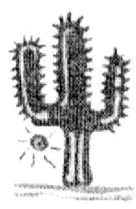

APPETIZERS

Appetizers:

Chile Stuffed Ripe Olives	12
BBQ Chicken Quesadillas	13-14
Pineapple Salsa	15-16
Papaya Salsa	17
Tostados (Corn Chips)	18
Quesadillas	19-20
Red Onion Olive Salsa	21-22
Nachos	23

CHILE STUFFED RIPE OLIVES

1 6 oz. can pitted ripe olives 1/4 tsp. oregano
1/4 c. olive oil   1 clove garlic, minced
1 T. wine vinegar   jalapeños, cut into strips
1 tsp. red chile flakes

Drain olives and combine with all ingredients except chiles. Let marinade, covered, 24-48 hours. When ready to serve, drain and stuff olives with chile strip.

BBQ CHICKEN QUESADILLAS

8 flour tortillas, 7-1/2"
4 oz. Monterey jack cheese grated
1 c. cooked chicken, shredded
4 green onions sliced

1-1/2 T parsley, chopped
12-14 fresh spinach leaves, washed and dried well
BBQ sauce (see pg. 155) or use bottled
4 oz. Cheddar cheese, grated

Put 4 tortillas on work surface and sprinkle with jack cheese. Scatter chicken, onions, parsley and bbq sauce
(more)

(continued)

over top. Cover with spinach leaves and sprinkle with Cheddar. Place a second tortilla over each and press down on tops with palm of hand to seal.

Heat a skillet with a little olive oil over medium heat and add a quesadilla. Pressing down with spatula and turning once when golden brown, about 3-4 minutes per side. Keep warm in low oven until ready to serve. Repeat with remaining quesadillas. To serve cut into quarters and serve hot with salsa, guacamole and sour cream on the side. For a zippier flavor, use jalapeño jack cheese.

PINEAPPLE SALSA

1 sm. pineapple, peeled and
   cored
3/4 c. red onion, minced
1 c. cilantro, chopped

1 T. rice vinegar
1/2 tsp. ground cayenne
salt to taste

Coarsely chop the pineapple and transfer to colander set
over a bowl to drain, about 5 minutes.

(more)

(continued)

Put pineapple in a bowl and add the onion, cilantro, vinegar, cayenne and a light sprinkling of salt. Stir to mix, cover and chill about 1 hour or as long as several hours. Excellent with chicken or fish.

PAPAYA SALSA

1 med. papaya, peeled, seeded and chopped
1 med. cucumber, seeded and chopped
1/2 c. red onion, chopped
1/4 c. cilantro, minced
1/4 c. vegetable oil
1/4 c. vinegar
2 packets sweetener
salt and pepper to taste

In a bowl, combine papaya, cucumber, onion and cilantro. In a small jar combine oil, vinegar, sweetener, salt and pepper and shake to mix well. Pour over papaya mixture and toss. Cover and chill

TOSTADOS (Corn Chips)

vegetable oil (shortening   garlic salt
   can be used if desired)   chile powder
12 corn tortillas   salt (optional)

Heat 2 inches of oil in a cast iron skillet over medium heat. Cut tortillas into quarters to within 1/2" from center of tortilla. Fry until crisp and drain on paper towels. Separate each tortilla into 4 tostados. These can be sprinkled with garlic salt, chile powder or any other seasoning you choose.

QUESADILLAS

4 tsp. vegetable oil	2 c. grated cheese
8 flour or corn tortillas	1 c. filling

Salsa, sour cream or guacamole for dipping

Heat a skillet over medium heat and add 1/2 t. oil.
When hot put 1 tortilla in pan, sprinkle with 1/4 c.
grated cheese, 1/4 c. filling, if using, and another 1/4 c.

(more)

(continued)

grated cheese. Top with second tortilla and cook until cheese is melted. Flip and cook until golden on both sides. Repeat with remaining ingredients. Cut into wedges and garnish with topping. Filling can be chicken, beef or anything you choose.

RED ONION OLIVE SALSA

3 med. red onions, skin on, halved   1 T. white wine vinegar
1/4 c. olive oil   1 tsp. red pepper flakes
1/4 c. balsamic vinegar   1 c. ripe olives, pitted
   2 T. oregano

Put onion halves, cut sides down in shallow pan and bake at 425° for 30 minutes or until onions are slightly soft when pinched and the cut sides are blackened. When cool enough to handle, discard skins and trim

(more)

(continued)

stems. Place onions in food processor or blender with oil, vinegars and red pepper flakes. Process in short bursts until just coarsely chopped. Add olives and oregano and process 2-4 seconds until chopped. Serve with tostados (see pg. 18) or small rounds of toasted bread.

NACHOS

50 tostados (see pg. 18)	1/2 c. sour cream
6 oz. Monterey Jack cheese	50 pcs. jalapeño chiles
cut into 1" cubes	red chile powder (optional)

Put tostados on a baking sheet and top each with a square of cheese. Spoon 1/2 tsp. sour cream and 1 piece of jalapeño on top. Sprinkle with chile powder. Heat in 450° oven 2-3 minutes or until cheese melts. Can be topped with chopped black olives and diced tomatoes if desired.

SOUPS

Soups:

Gazpacho	**26**
Albondigas Soup (Meatball Soup)	**27-28**
Arizona Potato Corn Chowder	**29-30**
Potato Soup	**31-32**
Green Chile Bisque	**33-34**

GAZPACHO

1/2 cucumber, peeled and
   diced
1/2 red onion, diced
1/2 avocado, peeled, pitted
   and sliced
ice cubes

1/2 tsp. oregano
3 T. olive oil
2 T. wine vinegar
4 c. canned tomato juice
2 limes, in wedges

Put vegetables and all other ingredients in a soup tureen
or bowl. Stir in tomato juice. Garnish with cucumber
and onion slices. When serving add a few ice cubes to
each bowl and a slice of lime.

ALBONDIGAS SOUP (Meatball Soup)

4 c. beef broth
2 c. tomatoes, diced
1 tsp. oregano
1/2 tsp. ground cumin
1/2 tsp. pepper
3/4 lb. ground beef

1/4 c. rice
1 egg
1/2 tsp. salt
1/2 c. green onions, thinly
    sliced
1/4 c. cilantro, chopped

In a large saucepan, over high heat, combine broth, tomatoes, including juice, 1/2 tsp. oregano, and 1/4 tsp. each cumin and pepper, cover and bring to a boil.

                                       (more)

(continued)

In a bowl, mix beef, rice, egg, salt and the remaining spices. When broth is boiling, drop beef mixture, in 1" balls into broth. Cover pan, reduce heat and simmer until rice in meatballs is tender to bite, about 10 minutes. Stir in green onions and cilantro.

ARIZONA POTATO CORN CHOWDER

14 sm. red potatoes, peeled
    and diced
1 can (17 oz.) cream corn
1 can (12 oz.) whole corn,
    undrained
2 chicken bouillon cubes
1/2 c. green chiles, diced
1 lg. onion, diced finely
1 green bell pepper, diced
salt and pepper to taste
dash garlic powder
dash Worcestershire sauce
2 c. Cheddar cheese, grated
1-1/2 c. Monterey jack
    cheese, grated

Cover potatoes with water and boil gently uncovered,

(more)

(continued)

until they are done. Add sautéed onion and green pepper. Stir in corns, chiles and seasonings and heat until bubbly. Turn to low heat and add cheeses and simmer for at least 1 hour. Serve with crusty warm bread or tortillas.

POTATO SOUP

4 strips bacon, diced	1 tsp. celery seed
4 c. potatoes, diced	salt and pepper to taste
2 8 oz. cans tomato paste	7 c. water
2 c. green chile, chopped	1 bay leaf
1/2 c. onion, finely chopped	1 clove garlic, chopped
1/2 tsp. cumin	oregano
grated cheese	

Fry bacon until crisp, drain and put aside. Roll potatoes

(more)

(continued)
in bacon drippings and put in large pan with all other
ingredients except, bacon, cheese and oregano. Simmer
for about 2 hours.

To serve place bacon, grated cheese and oregano in
bottom of soup tureen or bowl and pour soup over.
Serve with warmed tortillas.

GREEN CHILE BISQUE

1 32 oz. container mild
   green chile (found in
   in freezer section)
1 c. hot green chiles, diced
2 cans chicken broth
flour

1 white onion
oregano to taste
salt and pepper to taste
4 T. butter
1 T. garlic powder
1 qt. half and half

Combine mild and hot chiles and chicken broth and
blend in blender or food processor. Make a roux with

(more)

(continued)
butter and flour. Add browned roux paste to the chile
and blend again. Put chile mixture and half and half in
large pot and heat to just boiling. Serve hot over
crushed tostados (see pg. 18) and top with shredded
Monterey Jack cheese.

You can substitute regular milk for the half and half, it
won't be as rich.

NOTES:

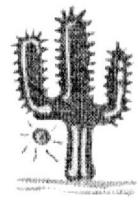

SALADS AND DRESSINGS

Salads and Dressings:

GREEN CHILE SALAD

1 T. vinegar
2 T. salad oil
1 clove garlic, cut
1 large tomato, diced

1 small onion, finely
   chopped
1/2 c. green chiles,
   roasted, seeded and
   chopped

Combine the vinegar and oil. Rub salad bowl with
garlic and add the tomato, onion and chiles. Let stand
for 30 minutes. Add dressing and toss gently. Serve on
lettuce leaves or great on cottage cheese. Serves 4.

BELL PEPPERS STUFFED WITH TOMATOES AND MOZZARELLA

3 red bell peppers
1-1/2 tsp. olive oil
1-1/2 T balsamic vinegar
1 clove garlic, minced

3/4 lb. cherry tomatoes,
  stemmed and halved
1 c. mozzarella, cubed
1/2 c. fresh basil leaves
  cut into thin strips

Cut peppers in half lengthwise and remove seeds and ribs. Cut a thin slice from the rounded side of each if necessary, to sit upright in baking dish.

(more)

(continued)

In a large bowl, whisk olive oil, vinegar, garlic and salt together. Add tomatoes, mozzarella and basil and mix well. Fill each pepper with mixture and bake at 375° until peppers are tender, about 40 minutes.

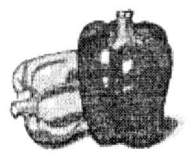

MOZZARELLA AND BELL PEPPER SALAD

6 oz. mozzarella cheese
1 jar roasted red peppers
1 small green bell pepper

2 T. olive oil
1/4 tsp. dried oregano
1/8 tsp. pepper

Slice cheese into 6 equal slices. Drain roasted peppers. Alternate cheese slices and roasted peppers on a serving platter. Remove stem and seeds from bell pepper and cut into thin rings. Arrange on platter with cheese and peppers. Drizzle with oil and sprinkle with oregano and pepper. Let stand until ready to serve. Serves 4.

CHILE PECAN DRESSING

1/2 c. vegetable oil

2 T. olive oil

2 T. lemon juice

1 T. honey

juice of 1 orange

2 T. green chile, chopped

1/2 c. pecans, finely
    chopped

Combine all ingredients except pecans in a blender and process. Add pecans and chill until ready to serve.

CHIPOTLE VINAIGRETTE

2 T. chipotle peppers,
   canned in adobo sauce
1 T. adobo sauce from can
1 T. brown sugar
1 tsp. sugar

1 tsp. cilantro
salt and pepper to taste
1/4 c. balsamic vinegar
1/4 c. fresh lime juice
1 c. olive oil

Combine peppers, sauce, brown sugar, sugar, cilantro, salt and pepper and set aside. Combine the vinegar and lime juice and whisk in the oil gradually. Pour over pepper mixture and stir well.

CILANTRO DRESSING

2 c. fresh cilantro, lightly packed	1/4 tsp. minced garlic
1/2 c. mayonnaise	1/4 tsp. grated lime peel
2 T. lime juice	1.4 tsp. salt
	1/8 tsp. pepper

Combine all ingredients in a blender or food processor until smooth. Store in refrigerator until ready to use.

SOUTHWESTERN SALAD DRESSING

1/4 c. lemon juice
1/4 c. water
1/2 c. olive oil
1 small onion
2 jalapeños

3 sprigs parsley
2 cloves garlic
1 tsp. cilantro
1/2 tsp. cumin
salt and pepper to taste

Combine all ingredients in blender or food processor
and process until onion and pepper are chopped fine.

VEGETABLES

Vegetables:

BAKED ONIONS WITH RAISINS AND PIÑONS

4 sweet onions	1/2 c. bread crumbs
1/4 c. clarified butter	1 T. seasoned salt
1/2 c. raisins, soaked in	1 T. sugar
warm water to plump	1/2 c. piñons, lightly toasted
1 T. sugar	1/2 c. chicken broth

Cut onions in half. Place 8 onion halves into a lightly greased, deep pan and sprinkle with raisins, piñons, bread crumbs, salt and sugar. Drizzle with butter and pour chicken broth into pan. Cover with foil and roast in a 375º oven for 30-40 minutes, until tender.

AVOCADO RELLENOS

3 lg. ripe avocados, peeled and pitted
2 tsp. lemon juice
1 tsp. lime juice
salt and pepper to taste
1/4 c. onion, minced
6 T. sour cream

3/4 c. Monterey Jack cheese grated
3 t. olive oil
5 green chiles, New Mexico or Anaheim, roasted and seeded

(more)

49

(continued)
In glass bowl, chop avocados, add the juices, salt, pepper, onion, cheese and oil and mix well. Stuff the mixture into the chiles and top each chile with sour cream. Serve at room temperature.

CORN SOUFFLÉ

1/4 c. butter or margarine	3 c. corn cut from cobs
1/4 c. flour	1 tsp. chile powder
1-1/2 tsp. salt	1/2 c. green chiles, chopped
1 T. sugar	6 eggs, separated
1-3/4 c. milk	

Melt butter in skillet and stir in flour, salt and sugar.
Cook until it starts to bubble then add milk and cook
over low heat. Let it thicken. Stir in corn and remove

(more)

(continued)

from heat. Let cool then stir in chile powder and chile. Beat egg yolks and stir into mixture. Beat whites until stiff and fold into mixture. Pour into a lightly greased soufflé dish and bake at 350° for 45 minutes, or until done. Serve immediately.

HOT STUFF CALABASAS

olive oil
1 sm. onion, diced
1 lg. zucchini or yellow
   summer squash
3 chiles, roasted, peeled
   seeded, and chopped

1 c. corn cut from cobs
1/2 c. Monterey Jack cheese
   grated
salt to taste

Heat oil in skillet and sauté onion until tender. Add

(more)

(continued)

squash, corn, salt and chile and toss until well coated with oil and onion. Transfer to casserole dish and sprinkle with cheese. Cover and bake at 350° for 30 minutes.

For a variation add fried bacon bits or fresh tomatoes.

MUSHROOM RELLENOS

25 med. mushrooms
6 green chiles, chopped
6 T. sour cream
1/4 tsp. garlic powder

black pepper
salt to taste
5 T. margarine or butter
5 T. sherry, divided

Remove mushroom stems and chop in to small pieces.
Combine with chiles. Add sour cream, garlic powder,
salt and pepper, 2 T. wine and 3 T. margarine or butter.
Mix thoroughly into a smooth paste. Stuff into
mushroom caps and mound.

(more)

(continued)

Pour remaining wine into a 12 x 9" baking dish and dot with remaining margarine. Add mushrooms to pan, cover and bake for 25 minutes.

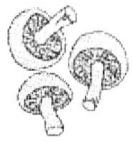

POSOLE

2 T. olive oil	1 tsp. salt
1 med. onion, finely chopped	1 tsp. oregano
2 cloves garlic, minced	2 tsp. ground cumin
1 lb. lean ground pork	1 c. green chiles, chopped
1 can (#10) white hominy with the juice	

Sauté onion and garlic in olive oil until soft. Stir in pork and add salt, oregano, cumin and chiles and cook

(more)

(continued)

until browned. Pour hominy with liquid into a large pot and stir in pork mixture and cook, covered over low heat, for one hour. Serve with red chile sauce (see pg. 163).

REFRIED BEANS

2 T. olive oil
1/2 c. juice from beans
salt to taste

4 c. cooked pinto beans
grated Cheddar cheese

Heat oil in heavy skillet and add beans and 1/2 c. of the juice. Cook over high heat and using a potato masher, mash beans as they cook, adding more liquid if necessary. When they form a thick paste, lower heat and simmer until ready to serve. Season with salt and pepper and sprinkle with cheese.

VEGETABLE RELISH

1 c. carrots, shredded
1 c. cucumber, chopped
1/2 c. red or green bell
   pepper, chopped
1/4 c. red onion, finely
   chopped

3 T. cider vinegar
1 tsp. sugar
salt to taste
1 T. olive oil

Combine all vegetables and set aside. Mix together vinegar, sugar and salt, then whisk in oil. Pour over vegetables and toss to coat. Cover and refrigerate at least 1 hour.

NOTES:

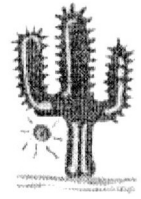

BREAD

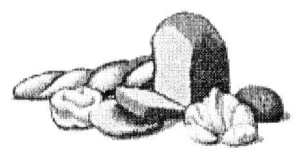

Bread:

JOSEFINAS (Toast with Chile Cheese)

1 slender baguette
1 c. jack cheese, grated
1 c. green chiles, diced
1/2 c. sweet onion, diced

1/2 c. sour cream
3 cloves garlic, minced
1/4 tsp. paprika

Cut baguette in half horizontally. In a bowl, mix cheese, chiles, onion, sour cream, garlic and paprika. Spread mixture, evenly, over sides of baguette and dust lightly with more paprika. Put on a baking sheet and broil 4 inches from heat until topping is puffy and lightly browned, about 6 minutes. Cut into 3/4" sections.

CHILE RED PEPPER BISCUITS

2-1/2 c. all purpose baking mix
1/2 tsp. crushed red pepper flakes
3/4 tsp. garlic powder, divided

1 c. milk
1 c. Cheddar cheese, grated
2 T. butter or margarine, melted

Combine baking mix, red pepper and 1/2 tsp. garlic powder. With fork stir in milk and cheese until mixture forms a soft dough. Drop dough by 1/4 c. onto greased

(more)

65

(continued)
cookie sheet. Combine butter or margarine and remaining garlic powder and brush on dough tops. Bake at 425° for 10-12 minutes or until golden brown.

GREEN CHILE ONION BREAD

6 6 oz. frozen loaves (thaw and rise type)	2 onions 1-1/2 c. green chiles, chopped

Remove loaves from freezer. spray with oil and cover with plastic wrap. Thaw overnight in refrigerator.

Julienne the onions and sauté in butter or margarine over medium heat until caramelized. Remove from heat

(more)

(continued)

and let cool. Add green chiles to onion mixture and mix well. Remove thawed loaves from refrigerator. Divide onion/chile mixture into 6 parts and cut into dough to incorporate. Reshape dough and let rise again. Bake for 30 minutes at the temperature listed on the bread dough.

FIESTA CORN BREAD

1-1/2 c. all purpose flour
6 tsp. baking powder
1/4 c. finely chopped
    green onion
1/4 c. sugar
1-1/2 c. yellow cornmeal
6 T. grated parmesan
    cheese

1/4 c. chopped green bell
    pepper
1 tsp. salt
6 T. melted butter
2 tsp. chile powder
1-1/3 c. milk
2 eggs, beaten

Sift flour, baking powder, salt and sugar. Add
                     (more)

(continued)

cornmeal, cheese, green pepper and onion. Melt butter with chile powder. Remove from heat. Pour milk mixture into flour mixture and stir until blended. Pour into a well greased 9" square pan and bake at 400° for 35 minutes. Cut into squares and serve hot.

FRY BREAD

3 c. flour

2 tsp. baking powder

1/2 tsp. salt

1 c. warm water

2 qts. vegetable oil

Mix dry ingredients together and pour in the warm water and mix. Knead until dough is soft but not sticky. You can add more flour or water as needed.

Put in bowl, cover and let sit for 15 minutes. Divide dough into 12 equal parts. Roll out until approximately 5 inches in diameter and 1/4 inch thick. Poke a hole in the middle. (more)

(continued)
Heat oil in heavy skillet and drop breads, one at a time into oil. Fry, turning until golden. Drain on paper towels.

NOTES:

MAIN DISHES

Main Dishes:

BRISKET

2-3 lb. brisket, trimmed   marinade of choice
bbq sauce of choice

Marinate brisket in your favorite marinade for at least
24 hours. This can be cooked several ways and all work
well. In a crockpot, place brisket, marinade and bbq
sauce and cook on low for 10-12 hours. Place in a
roasting pan, cover with marinade and bbq sauce, cover
with foil and bake for 3-4 hours. Or place on grill, with
                              (more)

(continued)

low heat, in a pan with marinade and bbq sauce and grill for 2-3 hours. This is a meat that needs slow cooking to be tender. It make take several tries to get it right but it is worth the trouble, it's delicious.

This can be made ahead of time, sliced and covered with sauce and reheated when ready to use.

CHERYL'S GREEN CHILE CHICKEN ENCHILADAS

1 chicken, cooked and
   shredded
1 can green enchilada
   sauce
1/2 c. green chiles, diced
1 can cream of chicken soup

chicken broth
flour tortillas
Monterey jack or jack
   and Cheddar combined

In a bowl combine enchilada sauce, chiles and cream of

(more)

(continued)
chicken soup. Add chicken broth to thin and season
with salt and pepper to taste and mix well. Put some of
this mixture on bottom of a baking dish.

Taking a flour tortilla, put in some chicken, shredded
cheese, a little of the sauce and roll up. Repeat until pan
is full. Pour balance of sauce over the rolled tortillas
and sprinkle with more cheese. Bake until cheese is
melted, about 30 minutes. Serve with sour cream,
guacamole and shredded lettuce. This can be made
ahead of time and frozen.

CHICKEN AND PORTABELLO MUSHROOMS

3 lg. portabello mushrooms
2-1/2 T. olive oil
salt and pepper to taste
1/2 c. chicken broth

4 chicken breasts, boneless
  and skinless
1/2 c. dry white wine
1/2 c. heavy cream

Clean mushrooms, arrange on a baking sheet and brush with some of the olive oil. Season with salt and pepper. Bake in a 425° oven for about 12-15 minutes or until tender. When cool, slice thinly and set aside.

(more)

(continued)

Sauté the chicken breasts in the remaining olive oil. Cook until well browned, and no longer pink. Transfer to a plate.

Add the white wine to skillet and boil over high heat, stirring to scrape up browned bits and reduced by half. Add chicken broth and reduce again. Add cream and continue to boil until reduced. Stir in mushrooms and add salt and pepper. Place chicken breasts on serving plate and cover with sauce. Serve with crusty bread and a green salad.

CHICKEN WITH MOLE SAUCE

4 chicken breasts, skinless
and boneless

olive oil

salt and pepper to taste

Mole Sauce:

2 bell peppers, seeded

1 tsp. anise seeds

2 T. sesame seeds

4 cloves garlic

3/4 c. pecans, shelled

2 corn tortillas, diced

2 oz. unsweetened chocolate, grated

6 roma tomatoes, peeled
and seeded

1/8 tsp. cloves, ground

1/4 tsp. cinnamon

salt to taste

1/2 tsp. cilantro

1/2 c. oil

2 c. chicken broth

(more)

(continued)
Sauté chicken breasts in olive oil until no longer pink.
Remove from pan and keep warm.

In the meantime, in a blender or food processor,
combine peppers, anise, sesame, garlic, pecans, tortillas
and tomatoes. Blend until smooth. Add spices and
process again. Add chocolate. Heat oil and add mixture
and then stock and simmer 20 minutes until thickened.
Make the day before for better flavor.

(more)

(continued)
Place chicken in a skillet and cover with mole sauce.
Simmer until breasts are heated through. Serve with
rice or noodles.

For Enchiladas:
Shred chicken, wrap in tortillas that have been softened
in microwave oven, cover with sauce, lettuce, diced
tomatoes, and other garnishes of your choice.

CHILE CON CARNE

1/2 c. onion, chopped
1 lb. ground beef
2 cans tomato sauce
2 c. pinto beans, cooked
2 c. water

1/2 tsp. garlic salt
salt to taste
1/4 c. red chile sauce
  (see pg. 163)

Sauté onion and beef in skillet with olive oil over medium heat until browned. Drain. Add remaining ingredients and simmer at low heat for 30 minutes. Use less red chile sauce for milder chile.

CHILE RELLENOS

8 long green chiles, roasted, seeded with stems on
8 pcs. Colby cheese in long strips to fit into chiles
1/2 c. flour
1 tsp. paprika
1/2 tsp. garlic powder
pinch of baking soda
3-4 eggs, well beaten
2-3 c. vegetable oil

Slit chiles lengthwise, being careful not to cut the top or bottom. Remove seeds and place a piece of cheese inside each. Fold one edge of opening into the other to form a seal. (more)

(continued)

Mix flour, paprika, garlic powder and baking soda. Dip chiles in beaten egg and dredge in flour mixture, then dip in egg mixture again. Heat oil in heavy skillet or deep fryer and fry chiles until golden brown. Drain on paper towels and serve at once.

CHILE STROGANOFF

olive oil

1 med. onion, chopped

1/2 c. mushrooms, sliced

2 lb. beef, cubed

2 c. beef broth

1/2 c. green chile, chopped

1 c. sour cream

1 pkg. 8 oz. noodles

Brown beef in olive oil. Remove from pan and add more oil if needed, and sauté onions, mushrooms and garlic until onions are soft. Put beef back in pan and add broth. Cover and simmer for 2 hours or until meat is

(continued)

tender. Add green chile and simmer for 10 minutes. Remove from heat and stir in sour cream.   Cook noodles according to package directions and serve stroganoff over noodles.

CHILE STUFFED CHICKEN BREAST

6 boneless chicken breasts
1/2 c. green chiles, chopped
2 oz. ham, minced
2 oz. Monterey Jack cheese
  shredded
1 clove garlic, minced
2 eggs, beaten
1 c. bread crumbs, seasoned
  with chile powder

Combine chiles with ham, cheese and garlic and set
aside at room temperature for about 15 minutes. Rinse
chicken and pat dry. Using a sharp knife cut a

(more)

(continued)

pocket in the side of each breast. Drain liquid out of stuffing mix and spoon about 1/6 of the mixture into each breast. Close with toothpicks. Dip breasts into beaten eggs and dredge in seasoned bread crumbs. Put into a greased 9 x 9" pan and bake at 350° for 45 minutes.

FAJITAS WITH PICO DE GALLO

1 lb. beef round or top
    sirloin

8 flour tortillas

Marinade:

2 T. fresh lime juice

2 T. olive oil

2 cloves garlic, crushed

Pico De Gallo:

1 c. tomato, seeded and
    chopped

1/4 c. salsa, prepared or
    your favorite homemade

1/2 c. zucchini, diced

1 T. fresh lime juice

1/4 c. fresh cilantro, chopped

(more)

93

(continued)
Put beef in plastic bag or large pan and cover with
marinade. Marinate in refrigerator for at least 1 hour.
In a medium bowl, combine Pico de Gallo ingredients
and mix well.

Remove steak from marinade, discard marinade and
place steak on rack in broiler pan or on grill. Cook until
medium rare. When finished, trim fat from steak and
cut crosswise into thin slices. Roll in tortillas with Pico
de Gallo.

FISH TACOS

1 lb. fresh fish, any mild fish   1 dz. sm. corn tortillas
    such as snapper, halibut
A variety of toppings:
       shredded lettuce or cabbage, any type
       diced tomatoes
       bell pepper slices, any color
       radishes, julienned
       cilantro, chopped
       salsa, a fruit salsa works well

(more)

(continued)

Grill or broil fish sprinkled with lime juice and salt and pepper until it flakes. Let cool slightly and shred. Warm tortillas and place a T. or so of the fish in the center. Garnish with your favorite toppings.

SOUTHWESTERN EGGS

1 bell pepper, chopped
1 lg. tomato, chopped
1 c. Cheddar cheese, grated
1 dz. eggs, well beaten

1 lg. onion, diced
3-4 jalapeño chiles,
   seeded and chopped
2 T. olive oil

Sauté onions and bell peppers in olive oil. Remove from the skillet and pour in beaten eggs and stir constantly until soft and very wet. Add all other ingredients. Serve at once. Serves 6. Good served with corn bread.

GREEN CHILE PIE

8 New Mexico or Anaheim
   green chiles, roasted
1/4 c. Cheddar cheese,
   grated

2 T. cream
salt and pepper to taste
6 eggs

Grease 10" pie plate. Slit chiles open lengthwise, remove seeds and stems and cover bottom of pie plate to form crust. Place remaining ingredients in blender and combine at low speed. Pour over chiles and bake at 325° for 30 minutes or until eggs are set.

GREEN CHILE QUICHE

1 can refrigerated crescent dinner rolls
1 c. whole green chiles, peeled and seeded
1 c. Monterey Jack cheese cubed

3 lg. eggs, beaten
3 T. milk
salt to taste
dash bottled hot sauce
2 tsp. parsley, chopped

Separate dough into 8 triangles. Place in an ungreased 8 or 9" pie plate, pressing pieces together to form a crust. Seal well. Cover bottom of crust with green chile and put cheese on top.   (more)

(continued)
Mix eggs, milk and seasonings and pour over top. Bake for 45-50 minutes or until edges are golden brown.

GREEN CHILE SOLE CASSEROLE

1 lb. mushrooms	3/4 c. chicken broth
2 T. olive oil	1/2 c. sour cream
1/2 c. onion, chopped	1 T. lime juice
1 c. green chiles, diced	1 lb. sole filets
2 T. flour	salt and pepper to taste

Clean mushrooms and remove stem ends, then thinly slice. Sauté in olive oil over high heat, stirring often until lightly browned. Spoon into a 1-1/2 qt. casserole. Add remaining oil and cook onions and chiles, stirring

(more)

(continued)

often, until onion is soft, about 5 minutes. Add flour and broth and mix well. Puree mixture in blender and return to pan.

Add sour cream and stir over high heat until boiling. Remove from heat and add lime juice. Rinse fish and pat dry. Place in an even layer over mushrooms in casserole and cover with sauce. Bake at 400° until fish flake, about 12 to 15 minutes. Season with salt and pepper.

HUEVOS RANCHEROS

8 corn or flour tortillas	8 eggs

1 lb. chorizo or pork
   sausage
	Cheddar or Colby cheese,
	   grated

red chile sauce (see pg. 163)	olive oil

Cook chorizo or pork sausage until browned. Heat oil in skillet and dip tortillas in quickly, one at a time, until soft, then drain on paper towels. The eggs can be cooked any way you like, but sunny side up makes a nice presentation. Heat red chile sauce in a saucepan.

(more)

(continued)

To Serve: Put 2 tortillas on a plate, spoon red chile sauce on them. Spoon drained sausage on top of sauce, then sprinkle with cheese. Put hot eggs to top it off and more chile sauce if desired.

Garnishes: Can be garnished with shredded lettuce, chopped tomatoes, diced black olives, avocado slices or anything that appeals to you.

MARTY'S RIGATONI WITH MUSHROOM SAUCE

1 T. unsalted butter
1/4 c. olive oil
1 lb. portabello mushrooms
2 cloves garlic, minced
1/4 tsp. red pepper flakes
1-1/2 c. chicken broth

1 chicken bouillon cube
1-1/2 T. parsley, chopped
salt to taste
1 lb. rigatoni or other pasta
1/4 c. parmesan, grated

Wipe mushrooms and grate. Melt butter and olive oil in large skillet. Add mushrooms, garlic and red pepper
(more)

(continued)

flakes. Sauté over medium heat until liquid from mushrooms evaporates, about 10 minutes. Add broth and bouillon cube and increase heat to high and cook 10 minutes. This allows flavors to blend. Remove from heat and stir in parsley and salt.

Cook pasta according to directions and drain well. Return to pot and add mushroom sauce. Stir over medium hear. Remove from heat and add parmesan and toss to mix.

MENUDO

5 c. tripe, well washed and trimmed

3 c. canned hominy, drained

6 qts. water

2 onions, minced

salsa

4 cloves garlic, minced and roasted

1 T. salt

1 tsp. oregano

1/2 c. green onions, minced

Cut tripe into slices about 1" wide and cook about 1

(more)

(continued)

hour in pan with water. Add hominy, onion, garlic, salt and oregano. Simmer 6 to 7 hours. To serve, top with green onions and salsa. This recipe serves about 18 but freezes well.

This is a highly spicy stew that is said to have medicinal powers, especially for hangovers, but is an acquired taste.

PORK CHOPS IN RED CHILE SAUCE

1 c. red chile sauce (see
   pg. 163)
salt to taste
2 cloves garlic, minced

1 tsp. oregano
4 boneless pork chops
2 T. olive oil

Mix seasonings with chile sauce and pour over pork
chops. Let marinate in refrigerator for at least 24
(more)

(continued)

hours. Remove chops from marinade and reserve.
Sauté chops in olive oil until brown on both sides. Pour
marinade over chops, cover and simmer for 30 minutes
or until chops are done.

PORTABELLA BURGERS

2 lg. egg whites

1 T. olive oil

1/3 c. Italian bread crumbs

2 T. chile powder

4 portabello mushroom caps,
    (save stems for other
    purposes)

4 round sandwich buns

1 c. sour cream

2 tsp. chiles, minced

1/4 c. red onion, thinly

1 c. spinach leaves, rinsed
    and dried

salt and pepper to taste

Beat egg whites and oil in bowl to blend. In another
bowl, mix crumbs and chile powder. Rinse and dry
mushroom caps. Coat each cap with egg mixture and
dip in crumbs. Set caps, gill sides down slightly apart on

(more)

111

(continued)

a 12 x 15" baking sheet. Lay bun halves, cut sides up, side by side on another baking sheet. Bake mushrooms in 450° oven until browned and flexible when pressed, about 20 minutes. About 3 minutes before mushrooms are done, add buns to oven and bake until lightly toasted.

In a small bowl, mix sour cream and chiles. Spread mixture on cut sides of buns. Layer equal amounts of onion and spinach on each bun and top with a mushroom. Salt and pepper to taste and cover with bun top.

SOUTHWEST BEEF STEW

3 lbs. beef round, cut into
   1" pieces
2 T. olive oil
salt and pepper to taste
1 c. beef broth
1 c. salsa, prepared or
   your favorite

2 med. zucchini, halved and
   cut crosswise into 1" pcs.
1 15 oz. can black beans,
   drained
1/2 c. fresh corn kernels
2 T. cornstarch

In heavy skillet, heat oil and cook beef, over medium
(more)

(continued)

heat until browned. Season with salt and pepper. Stir in broth and salsa and bring to a boil. Reduce heat to low and cover and simmer for 1-1/2 hours.

Stir in zucchini, beans and corn and bring to a boil again. Reduce heat, cover and simmer for another 20 minutes, until tender. Mix cornstarch with water and stir into mixture. Cook until thickened. Top with sour cream or Jack cheese.

SOUTHWESTERN LASAGNA

1 lb. ground beef
1 can 10 oz. red enchilada
  sauce
1/4 c. ripe olives, pitted
  and sliced
1/2 c. green chile, chopped

1 can 16 oz. tomatoes
1/2 c. oil
8 corn tortillas
4 oz. Cheddar cheese
salt to taste

Cook ground beef until no longer pink. In saucepan, combine tomatoes, enchilada sauce, olives, chiles and salt. Add ground beef mixture and simmer covered for

(more)

(continued)
20 minutes, stirring occasionally.

Cut two tortillas into quarters and cook in oil until crisp. Drain and set aside. Break up remaining tortillas. Spread 1/3 of meat mixture into a 9" baking dish. Top with 1/2 cheese, then 1/2 broken tortillas. Repeat layers ending with meat mixture. Top with quartered tortillas and bake at 350° for 30 minutes. Sprinkle more cheese over top and heat until cheese melts. Let stand for 5 minutes before serving.

STUFFED SOPAIPILLAS
(Sopaipillas Rellenos)

6 sopaipillas (see pg. 137) 2 c. red chile sauce (see
1-1/2 c. ground beef, cooked   pg. 163)
1 med. onion, chopped   shredded lettuce (optional)
1-1/2 c. Cheddar cheese   chopped tomatoes (optional)
  grated

Cut a slit along one side of the sopaipillas. Fill with
ground beef, onion and cheese. Put in casserole dish and
cover with chile sauce and cheese and bake at 350° for

(more)

(continued)
about 15 minutes or until cheese is melted and sauce is
hot. Garnish with lettuce and tomatoes.

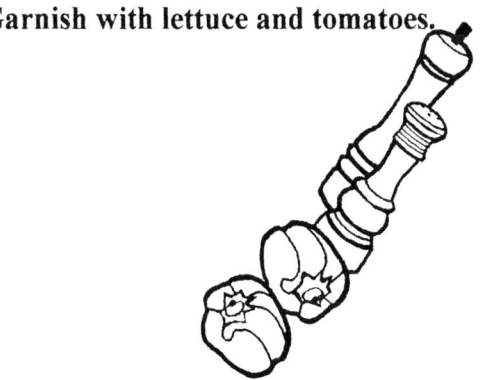

TAMALES

Masa Dough:

1-1/3 c. lard, vegetable
   shortening, or butter
2 c. masa harina

2 tsp. salt
2-2/3 c. chicken broth

Whip shortening until fluffy and add masa flour, salt and broth until it holds together. Cover with a damp cloth and keep cool until ready to use. This is enough for about 40 tamales.

(more)

(continued)
Fillings:
Beef :

1 lb. ground beef	1/2 c. red chile sauce, (see
1 med. onion, chopped	pg.) or use canned
	enchilada sauce

Brown ground beef and add onion and cook until soft. Add chile sauce and cover and simmer for 10 minutes, stirring occasionally. Makes about 3 cups.

(more)

(continued)

Chorizo:

1 lb. chorizo, skinned	1/2 tsp. cumin
1 lg. onion, finely chopped	1/4 tsp. cinnamon
2 tsp. each chile powder	1 tsp. salt
and oregano	5 T. vinegar
1-1/2 c. canned enchilada	hot pepper seasoning
sauce	if desired

Crumble chorizo and cook until brown. Add onion and cook until soft. Add seasonings and mix well. Pour in enchilada sauce and cook, uncovered, until boiling and most liquid is gone.   (more)

(continued)

Chicken or Pork:

2 c. chicken, turkey or pork, cooked and shredded

1 med. onion, chopped

1-1/2 T oil

1 small jalapeño, minced

1/4 c. raisins

1-1/2 T. ripe olives, chopped

2/3 c. red chile sauce (see pg. 166) or canned enchilada sauce

Sauté onion until soft. Stir in meat, chile, raisins, olives and chile sauce. Simmer uncovered for 10 minutes, stirring occasionally. (more)

(continued)
This is just a sample of the fillings you can use. It's a matter of what tastes good to you. There are other fillings in this book that would work equally as well. Experiment and you'll find the one you like best.

Each of the above recipes makes about 3 cups of filling. To make 40 tamales, double the recipes.

Corn Husks:
These can be purchased in dried form in any

(more)

(continued)

grocery or specialty stores that handle Mexican foods. If husks are not available you can use foil or plastic wrap. These materials however do not give the authentic corn flavor that makes truly great tamales.

To use, soak husks in warm water for about 2 hours or overnight so that they are pliable. Keep damp until ready to use.

(more)

(continued)

Filling and Folding:

Choose a corn husk and lay flat on working surface with tip away from you. Spread 2 T. masa dough in a rectangle about 5" across by 4" down. Leave margins of at least 2-3" at bottom, 1" at top and 1" or more on left. If the husk is not wide enough to accommodate dough, use 2 husks with masa dough to paste them together.

Spoon 2 T. filling into the center of the masa, then begin
(more)

(continued)

folding. Fold right side over center, then left side over filling, allowing the uncovered part of the husk to wrap around tamale. Fold bottom over dough enclosed filling, then fold down the tip of the husk, wrapping it around the tamale. Lay fold side down to keep it closed. If you wish, it can be tied with a strip of husk about 1/4" wide.

Steaming:

You can steam in a bamboo steamer, roasting pan with cover, or anyway you like. All you need is a rack above at least 1" of boiling water.   (more)

(continued)

Stack tamales loosely on a rack, folded side down. This will help the steam to circulate around and cook them evenly. Cover and boil gently, adding more water as needed, for about 45 minutes to one hour.

After the time allotted, test to see if they are done. They are done if the masa dough is firm and doesn't stick to the husk.

Tamales can be cooked ahead and frozen. To reheat, steam unfrozen or put in microwave oven until warmed through.

DESSERTS

Desserts:

CHIMICHANGAS

12 flour tortillas
oil for deep frying
powdered sugar

2 c. prepared fruit pie
filling or jam

Spoon 3 T. of filling or jam down the middle of each tortilla. Fold in ends of tortilla then roll up like an egg roll and secure with a toothpick. Drop the chimichangas into hot oil one or two at a time and fry until golden brown. Drain and lightly dust with powdered sugar.

DESSERT TAMALES

1/2 recipe tamale masa (see pg. 119)
1/2 c. sugar
1 tsp. cinnamon

1/2 c. pistachios, ground
12 corn husks, (see pg. 123)
3/4 c. raisins

Combine the prepared masa, sugar, cinnamon and pistachios in a bowl. Spread about 3 T. masa mixture down the center of each soaked corn husk and top the mixture with raisins. Fold the husks (see pg. 125) and set aside. When ready to use, steam, covered over boiling water about 45 minutes.

(continued)
These can be made ahead of time and frozen for up to 6 months. Just thaw and steam.

A variation is to spread masa mixture with 2 tsp. preserves.

ORANGE BISCOTTI COOKIES

2 c. flour
1/2 c. sugar
4 tsp. baking powder
1/2 tsp. salt
1/2 tsp. cream of tartar

1/2 c. butter
1 egg, slightly beaten
1 c. milk
2 t. grated orange peel
1/2 tsp. anise, powdered

In a bowl, sift together flour, sugar, baking powder, salt and cream of tartar. Cut the shortening into the flour until the mixture resembles coarse crumbs.

(more)

(continued)

Mix egg and milk and add this to dry mixture. Stir until dough is just mixed and place on a floured surface. Mix in orange peel and anise and knead gently for 30-60 seconds. Drop dough onto a greased cookie sheet by the teaspoonful. Bake for 12 to 15 minutes.

PECAN PIE SOUTHWESTERN STYLE

5 eggs
1 c. light corn syrup
1 c. maple syrup
1 tsp. vanilla
1 c. pecans, coarsely
    chopped

1/4 c. flour
2 T. butter, melted
1/4 tsp. salt
9 inch unbaked pie shell,
    deep dish

Beat eggs well. Add all remaining ingredients except
(more)

(continued)

pecans and pie shell and beat. Pour into unbaked shell and sprinkle pecans over the top. Push pecans down into the mixture. Bake at 425° for 15 minutes, then reduce heat to 350° and bake for another 30 minutes or until set. Decorate top with whole pecans.

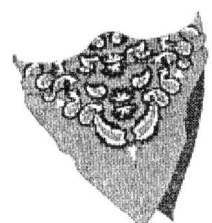

SOPAIPILLAS

2 c. flour	1-1/2 T vegetable oil (1 T.
2 tsp. baking powder	lard can be substituted)
1 tsp. salt	warm water
1 tsp. sugar	oil for deep frying

Mix flour with baking powder, salt and sugar. Pour in oil and mix with your fingers to combine. Add water working into flour until a sticky dough forms. Put into a covered bowl and let stand at room temperature for 30 minutes.   (more)

(continued)
Roll out dough on a floured board to 1/8 inch thickness. Cut into 3 inch triangles and fry in hot oil until fluffy and golden brown. Drain on paper towels. Serve with honey butter.

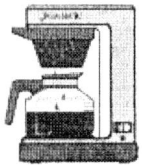

SOUTHWESTERN PRALINES

1 c. brown sugar
2 c. sugar
3 T. light corn syrup
1/4 tsp. salt

1 c. heavy cream
4 T. butter or margarine
2 tsp. maple flavoring
1-1/2 c. pecan halves

Oil a large saucepan on the inside and combine the
sugars, corn syrup, salt, cream and butter or margarine.
Cook slowly over medium heat until mixture reaches the
medium firm ball stage. Remove from heat.

(more)

(continued)
Let cool. Add the flavoring and pecans and beat until
creamy. Drop by spoonfuls onto wax paper. If mixture
hardens, add a few drops of cream and heat until
creamy.

SPICY PECANS

1 T. olive oil	3/4 tsp. cumin
2 T. butter or margarine	1/2 tsp. paprika
1 T. Worcestershire sauce	1/2 tsp. garlic powder
2 c. pecans	1/2 tsp. Tabasco
1 tsp. salt	

Heat oil and butter or margarine in a sauce pan. Add the remaining ingredients, except nuts and salt. Simmer over low heat for 3-4 minutes to blend.   (more)

(continued)
Add nuts and toss to coat. Spread on a baking sheet and
bake for 15 minutes in a 325° oven, shaking occasionally.
Toss with salt and let cool to room temperature. Store
in an air tight container.

STRAWBERRY MARGARITA PIE

1-1/4 c. pretzels, finely
   crushed
2/3 c. butter or margarine
1/4 c. sugar
1 env. unflavored gelatin
1/2 c. sugar

2 eggs, separated
1/4 c. tequila
1/4 c. frozen strawberries
1 c. whipping cream
1/4 c. lime juice
strawberries for decoration

Lightly oil a 9" pie plate. Combine pretzels, butter or margarine and 1/4 c. sugar. Press firmly on bottom and up sides of pie plate. Refrigerate. Sprinkle gelatin over

(more)

(continued)

lime juice in small pan and add 1/4 c. sugar and egg yolks. Stir to blend and cook over low heat, stirring constantly until gelatin dissolves and mixture thickens.

Remove from heat and stir in tequila and strawberries. Refrigerate, stirring occasionally until mixture is thick. Beat egg whites until stiff, and gradually beat in balance of sugar. Fold into gelatin mixture. Whip cream and fold into gelatin mixture. Spoon into crust, cover and refrigerate until firm. Decorate with strawberries.

NOTES:

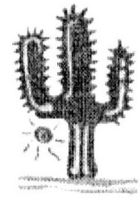

MISCELLANEOUS

Miscellaneous:

AVOCADO BUTTER

1/2 tsp. serrano chile,
   minced
2 tsp. lime juice
1 stick unsalted butter

1/3 c. avocado, chopped
1 T. fresh cilantro
salt to taste

Put chile and lime juice in a small saucepan and bring to a boil. Simmer for 30 seconds and remove from heat to cool. Put cooled mixture with the remaining ingredients in a bowl and, using a fork or electric mixer, blend into a paste. Good basted on fish.

APPLE CHUTNEY

3 ea. red and green bell
   peppers
12 tart apples
12 med. tomatoes
6 med. onions
1 c. celery, diced

2 oz. ginger, crystallized
1 lb. seedless raisins
2 qts. cider vinegar
3 c. sugar
2 tsp. salt

Cut peppers into halves and remove seeds. Pare apples

(more)

(continued)
and remove core. Chop vegetables, apples, ginger and raisins in food processor or blender. Combine all ingredients in large pan and cook until thick and clear, about 1 hour.

CHILE VERDE CHUTNEY

1 c. cider vinegar
1 c. brown sugar
6 oz. tomatillos, husked
   and chopped
1 med. onion, minced

3/4 c. New Mexico or
   Anaheim chile, roasted,
   seeded and peeled
1/2 tsp. ground cumin
salt to taste

Combine all ingredients in saucepan and simmer over medium heat until cooked down and thick, about 30-45 minutes. This can be used immediately or transferred to a jar and refrigerated for up to 2 weeks.

(more)

(continued)
This is great on biscuits or cornbread, Also used as a
glaze for vegetables or fish.

MANGO BUTTER

2-1/2 tsp. lime juice
1/2 tsp. lime peel, minced
1/2 tsp. orange peel
1/2 stick unsalted butter
1/4 tsp. nutmeg

1/2 tsp. chile powder
1/3 c. mango, peeled, seeded
  and minced
1/8 tsp. cinnamon
salt to taste

Place lime juice, lime peel and orange peel in a small saucepan and bring to a boil. Simmer for 30 seconds and remove from heat to cool. Put cooled mixture with the remaining ingredients and using a fork or electric mixer, blend to a paste.

ARIZONA CILANTRO PESTO

2 c. cilantro, tightly packed   3 garlic cloves
1 jalapeño, diced   1/2 c. pistachio nuts
3/4 c. Parmesan cheese   3/4 c. olive oil
salt and pepper to taste

Put cilantro, jalapeño and garlic in food processor or blender and process to a fine paste. Add nuts and cheese and blend again. Slowly pour olive oil into mixture a little at a time and blend until smooth and creamy. Stores for a short time in refrigerator, also freezes well.

CHIPOTLE PINEAPPLE BBQ SAUCE

2 T. olive oil
1 c. onion, chopped
1 c. red bell pepper, diced
1 c. chicken broth
1 c. fresh pineapple,
   chopped
2 T. chipotle peppers

3/4 c. tomato paste
1/2 c. dark corn syrup
1/2 c. pineapple juice
2 T. soy sauce
2 T. honey
1 T. Dijon mustard
2 T. cider vinegar

Sauté onions and bell peppers in olive oil. Add broth,
(more)

(continued)

pineapple and chipotle peppers. Remove from pan and puree, then return to pan and add rest of ingredients. Cool until heated through. Great on chicken or pork.

CHILE TOMATO SAUCE

16 green chiles, roasted,
    peeled
1/4 tsp. garlic powder
salt to taste
1 lb. ground beef
2 T. olive oil

1/4 c. onion, chopped
2-1/2 T. flour
2 c. tomatoes, chopped
2-1/2 c. water
6 jalapeño peppers, diced
    (optional)

In bowl, mix chiles with garlic powder and salt and set
aside. In skillet, brown beef and drain. In separate pan,
(more)

(continued)
sauté onions, in oil. When slightly browned, add flour
and make a smooth paste. Gradually stir in tomatoes
with juice, the chile mixture and water. Stir in browned
meat and simmer for 5 minutes. Add jalapeños to taste.

This is a great sauce for tacos, enchiladas or as a stew
by itself. The amount of jalapeños you add makes the
degree of hotness.

GREEN CHILE SAUCE

3 T. vegetable oil
1 lg. onion
3 cloves garlic, minced
2 T. flour
1 tsp. salt

2 c. New Mexican green
    chiles, roasted and
    chopped
2 c. chicken broth
1 tsp. cilantro, chopped

Heat oil in saucepan over medium heat. Add onion and
sauté until soft, 5 minutes. Stir in garlic and sauté

(more)

(continued)

another minute. Add flour and continue cooking for a few more minutes. Mix in the chile, broth and add seasonings. Bring to a boil, then reduce heat and simmer 10-15 minutes, until thick.

This sauce keeps for about 1 week and freezes well.

TEQUILA MINT SAUCE

1/2 c. tequila
2 tsp. lime juice
1 tsp. garlic, minced
salt to taste
1 tsp. serrano chile, minced
chile powder (optional)

2 tsp. mint sauce
1 T. onion, minced
1/4 c. heavy cream
6 T. butter, cut into small
  pieces
mint leaves (optional)

Mix all ingredients except cream, butter and chile
powder in a saucepan and bring to a boil over medium
(more)

(continued)
heat. Stir in cream and continue boiling until the mixture begins to thicken, 4-5 minutes. Remove from heat and stir in butter. Sprinkle with chile powder. Great served over chicken or fish.

RED CHILE SAUCE

30-35 red chile pods   salt to taste
5 c. water

Rinse chile and remove seeds and stems. Put chile in a saucepan and cover with water. Bring to a boil. Lower heat and simmer for at least 15 minutes. Let cool and process in food processor or blender. Strain through a sieve and add salt. Store for a short time in the refrigerator, can be frozen. This is a basic red chile sauce that has many uses.

ARIZONA SUNSET

1-1/2 oz. tequila   1 oz. grenadine**
6 oz. fresh orange juice   ice cubes

Combine all ingredients in a cocktail shaker. Pour into
frosted glass and garnish with a slice of the orange.

**This can be substituted with prickly pear syrup which
can be found in specialty liquor stores.

MARGARITAS

6 oz. tequila
6 oz. triple sec
coarse salt
crushed ice

6 oz. lime juice

In a blender, combine tequila, triple sec, lime juice and ice. Blend until frothy. Chill stemmed glasses and invert rims in salt to coat evenly. Pour blended mixture into chilled glasses.

GLOSSARY

Avocados - A wonderful addition to any dish. This creamy fruit is a counterpoint to the hot chiles. For best results when using in salsa or any other dish, combine all ingredients first then add avocado at the last minute. Lime juice will prevent discoloration.

Beans (Frijoles) - Beans are one of the most important ingredients of southwestern cooking. Among the varieties are:

Black Beans - A very dark purple bean.

Pinto Beans - The most common, these are native of the southwestern U.S. Pinto means painted.

White Beans - Known also as navy beans.

Blue Corn - A variety of corn used in the southwest for centuries. It has a strong flavor and is used much the same way as yellow or white corn.

Burrito - A flour tortilla rolled up to enclose a filling.

Calabasa - **A Mexican squash. Can be substituted with zucchini.**

Cheese (Queso) - **Used in many southwestern dishes. The following are some of the most popular:**

Monterey Jack - **A creamy, flavorful cheese. Other jack cheeses can be used, but Monterey is the best variety.**

Yellow or White Cheddar - **A hard cheese good in all dishes.**

Asadero Cheese - **A semi-soft white cheese that is popular in northern New Mexico. A good substitute for Monterey Jack or Mozzarella.**

Queso Fresco - **A traditional Mexican cheese, somewhat like feta. It may be found at Mexican markets.**

Chile Relleno - **A chile filled with some type of stuffing,**

Chimichanga - **A deep fried burrito.**

Chorizo - **A spicy sausage.**

Cilantro - Also known as coriander or Chinese parsley. This is a wonderful spice that can be used in almost anything.

Corn Husks - Used as a wrapper in which to cook food. Usually used to make tamales.

Enchiladas - A casserole with soft tortillas and filled with cheeses, meat, chicken or fish and topped with a sauce.

Fajitas - Strips of marinated meat or chicken sautéed quickly and served with tortillas, grilled onions, peppers, salsa, guacamole and sour cream.

Hominy - Corn kernels soaked in a lime solution. Used in chiles and the main ingredient in posole.

Jicama - A potato-like vegetable used in salads.

Masa - Corn flour that has been treated and is used to make tortillas and tamales.

Maíz - Corn

Nopales - A prickly pear cactus pad available in jars in southwest food sections. They should be rinsed before using.

Piñons - A nut of the pine tree.

Quesadillas- A fried or grilled tortilla with a filling.

Sopapilla - A deep fried, puffy bread usually served as a dessert.

Tamale - Masa with a filling and wrapped in corn husks and steamed until cooked.

Tomatillos - A member of the gooseberry family, these have a papery outer husk which must be peeled off. There is a sticky residue that has to be washed off with hot water before using. These can be used cooked or raw and add a tart flavor to any dish.

Tomatoes - Many of us cannot find good tomatoes all year round so when in doubt use Roma or plum tomatoes. These are meaty varieties and are especially good roasted, bringing out their full flavor.

Tostadas - Fried tortilla served flat and topped with a variety of mixtures.

NEED GIFTS?

Are you up a stump for some nice gifts for some nice people in your life? Here's a list of some of the best cookbooks in the western half of the Universe. Just check 'em off, stick a check in an envelope with this page, and we'll get your books off to you pronto. Oh, yes, add $2.00 for shipping and handling for the first book and then fifty cents more for each additional one. If you order over $30.00, forget the shipping and handling.

Mini Cookbooks

(Only 3 1/2 x 5) With Maxi Good Eatin' - 160 or 192 pages - $5.95

- ❏ Arizona Cooking
- ❏ Dakota Cooking
- ❏ Illinois Cooking
- ❏ Indiana Cooking
- ❏ Iowa Cookin'
- ❏ Kansas Cookin'
- ❏ Kentucky Cookin'
- ❏ Michigan Cooking
- ❏ Minnesota Cookin'
- ❏ Missouri Cookin'
- ❏ New Jersey Cooking
- ❏ New Mexico Cooking
- ❏ New York Cooking
- ❏ Ohio Cooking
- ❏ Pennsylvania Cooking
- ❏ Wisconsin Cooking
- ❏ Amish Mennonite Apple Cookbook
- ❏ Amish Mennonite Pumpkin Cookbook
- ❏ Amish & Mennonite
   Strawberry Cookbook
- ❏ Apples! Apples! Apples!
- ❏ Apples Galore
- ❏ Berries! Berries! Berries!
- ❏ Berries Galore!
- ❏ Bountiful Blueberries

- ❏ Cherries! Cherries! Cherries!
- ❏ Citrus! Citrus! Citrus!
- ❏ Cooking with Cider
- ❏ Cooking with Fresh Herbs
- ❏ Cooking with Spirits
- ❏ Cooking with Garlic
- ❏ Cooking with Things Go Baa
- ❏ Cooking with Things Go Cluck
- ❏ Cooking with Things Go Moo
- ❏ Cooking with Things Go Oink
- ❏ Cooking with Things Go Splash
- ❏ Crockpot Cookbook
- ❏ Good Cookin' From the
   Plain People
- ❏ Hill Country Cookin'
- ❏ Holiday & Get-together Cookbook
- ❏ How to Make Salsa
- ❏ Kid Cookin'
- ❏ Kid Fun
- ❏ Kid Money
- ❏ Kid Pumpkin Fun Book
- ❏ Midwest Small Town Cookin'
- ❏ Muffins Cookbook
- ❏ Nuts! Nuts! Nuts!
- ❏ Off To College Cookbook

- ❏ Peaches! Peaches! Peaches!
- ❏ Pumpkins! Pumpkins! Pumpkins!
- ❏ Some Like It Hot
- ❏ Squash Cookbook
- ❏ Super Simple Cookin'
- ❏ Working Girl Cookbook
- ❏ Veggie Talk Coloring &
   Story Book $6.95

In-Between Cookbooks

(5 1/2 x 8 1/2) - 150 pages - $9.95

- ❏ Amish Ladies Cookbook - Old
   Husbands
- ❏ Amish Ladies Cookbook - Young
   Husbands
- ❏ The Adaptable Apple Cookbook
- ❏ Bird Up! Pheasant Cookbook
- ❏ Breads! Breads! Breads!
- ❏ Camp Cookin'
- ❏ Civil War Cookin',
   Stories, 'n Such
- ❏ Cooking Ala Nude
- ❏ Cooking for a Crowd
- ❏ Country Cooking
   Recipes from my Amish Heritage
- ❏ The Cow Puncher's Cookbook
- ❏ Eating Ohio
- ❏ Farmers Market Cookbook
- ❏ Feast of Moons Indian Cookbook
- ❏ Fire Fighters Cookbook
- ❏ Football Mom's
- ❏ Halloween Fun Book
- ❏ Herbal Cookery

- ❑ Hunting in the Nude Cookbook
- ❑ Ice Cream Cookbook
- ❑ Indian Cooking Cookbook
- ❑ Little 'Ol Blue-Haired Church-Lady Cookbook
- ❑ Mad About Garlic
- ❑ Make the Play All-Sport Cookbook
- ❑ Motorcycler's Wild Critter Cookbook
- ❑ Outdoor Cooking for Outdoor Men
- ❑ Shhh Cookbook
- ❑ Soccer Mom's Cookbook

- ❑ Southwest Ghost Town Cookbook
- ❑ Turn of the Century Cooking
- ❑ Vegan Vegetarian Cookbook
- ❑ Venison Cookbook

Biggie Cookbooks

(5 1/2 x 8 1/2) - 200 plus pages - $11.95

- ❑ A Cookbook for them what Ain't Done a Whole lot of Cookin'
- ❑ Aphrodisiac Cooking
- ❑ Back to the Supper Table Cookbook
- ❑ Cooking for One (ok, Maybe two)

- ❑ Covered Bridges Cookbook
- ❑ Depression Times Cookbook
- ❑ Dial-a-Dream Cookbook
- ❑ Flat Out, Dirt Cheap Cookin'
- ❑ Hormone Helper Cookbook
- ❑ Real Men Cook on Sunday Cookbook
- ❑ The I-got-Funner-things-to do Cookbook
- ❑ Victorian Sunday Dinners

HEARTS 'N TUMMIES COOKBOOK CO.

1854 - 345th Avenue

Wever, Iowa 52658

1-800-571-BOOK

Name _____

Address _____

_____

*You Iowa folks gotta kick in another 6% for Sales Tax.